EASY SOLOING
for Blues Keyboard
Fun Lessons for Beginning Improvisers

TRICIA WOODS

Alfred, the leader in educational publishing, and the National Guitar Workshop, one of America's finest guitar schools, have joined forces to bring you the best, most progressive educational tools possible. We hope you will enjoy this book and encourage you to look for other fine products from Alfred and the National Guitar Workshop.

Alfred Publishing Co., Inc.
16320 Roscoe Blvd., Suite 100
P.O. Box 10003
Van Nuys, CA 91410-0003
alfred.com

ISBN-10: 0-7390-4808-2 (Book & CD)
ISBN-13: 978-0-7390-4808-5 (Book & CD)

This book was acquired, edited and produced
by Workshop Arts, Inc., the publishing arm of
the National Guitar Workshop.
Nathaniel Gunod, acquisitions, managing editor
Burgess Speed, senior editor
Matthew Liston, editor
Timothy Phelps, interior design
Ante Gelo, music typesetter
CD recorded by Greg Buford at Kobe Studio, West Orange, NJ
Tricia Woods (keyboard); Gregory Jones (bass); Greg Buford (drums)
Cover photograph: © SXC.HU

TABLE OF CONTENTS

 A compact disc is included with this book. This disc can make learning with the book easier and more enjoyable. The symbol shown at the left appears next to every example that is on the CD. Use the CD to help ensure that you're capturing the feel of the examples, interpreting the rhythms correctly, and so on. The track number below the symbol corresponds directly to the example you want to hear.

ABOUT THE AUTHOR

Tricia Woods grew up in northern New York and performed as a pianist and vocalist from an early age. She studied at Brown University, Cornish College of the Arts, and New York's City College, where she earned a master's degree in piano performance. While in the Northwest, she led several original groups, was featured at Seattle's Bumbershoot Festival, and received critical acclaim as an artist to watch. Tricia moved to New York in 1995, where she continued to compose, arrange, and perform. She has toured with Savion Glover in *Bring in 'Da Noise, Bring in 'Da Funk*, appeared on CNN's *That's Entertainment*, and worked extensively with her own trios and quartets as well as groups such as Jeff Newell's New-Trad Octet and Hayes Greenfield's Jazz-A-Ma-Tazz.

PHOTO BY JERRY MOSS

Tricia is a committed teacher as well as performer. She teaches individual lessons and is a faculty member of Jazz Connections, Montclair, New Jersey's highly acclaimed jazz program for youth. She has taught at the Brooklyn Conservatory of Music and the National Keyboard Workshop. She has also taught over one thousand New York City children, through classroom programs such as The Musical Theatre Foundation, Brooklyn Conservatory's Music Partners, and Create! She has authored two blues piano books published by Alfred/NGW: *Beginning Blues Keyboard* (#22621) and *Intermediate Blues Keyboard* (#18418).

Acknowledgements

This book is dedicated to all who embark on the journey of discovering your own musical voice through blues improvisation. A debt of gratitude is owed to each of you for continuing the legacy of the great artists who have expressed themselves through this music that we call the blues. Particularly, I owe a great deal to all of the students with whom I've worked over the years. You have continually helped to shape my ideas about music and you are the source of the ideas, exercises, and methods in this book. Thanks to my family, both immediate and extended, for always making music a part of daily life, and especially to Gregory and Christopher for reminding me of the importance of "hearing" the music. Deepest gratitude to the musicians and administrators who have continued to encourage, support, and influence my efforts to study and teach blues and jazz: Jeff Newell and the New-Trad Octet, Peter Fand and Create!, Janet Lemansky and Jazz Connections, Jim Buchanan, and many others. Thanks and respect go to Greg Buford (drums and recording) and Gregory Jones (bass) for contributing their excellent musicianship and spirit to this recording, and to Jerry Moss for his photography. Finally, thanks to Burgess Speed, Workshop Arts, and Alfred Publishing for facilitating this work and for allowing musical integrity to be the guiding factor throughout the project.

INTRODUCTION

Improvising, soloing, jamming, riffing, spontaneous composition—they all mean the same thing: making music in the moment that is uniquely your own. For many musicians, it's the best part of playing music, a chance to be fun, creative, and expressive. But for some, it can be intimidating. How do I know what to play? What if no one likes it? What if I get lost in the form? These are all valid concerns, but not great enough to overpower the excitement of improvising. This book is designed to help you do just that.

The blues are a great vehicle for learning improvisation. Many forms of music are influenced by the blues, including jazz, R&B, funk, rock, bossa nova, and zydeco. Listen to musicians soloing in any of these genres, and you'll hear the influence of the blues. The blues is a vocal- and lyric-based music. It has always been about *saying* something. Whether you're singing, bending a guitar string, or striking a cluster of notes on the piano, you're "talking" when you play the blues—and that is really what soloing is all about. Most blues music is based on a short, easily recognizable form. This makes the process of developing ideas into solos a manageable task.

Whether you are a beginner or an experienced musician who's new to soloing, you will find something inspirational in this book. If you're new to the blues, pages 5–12 will acquaint you with the chords and left-hand techniques you'll need. If you're already familiar with the blues, you can get right to the task of soloing.

Beginning on page 13, you will learn to solo. Each new concept will be accompanied by both written and listening exercises. The listening exercises are designed to keep your ears up to speed with what your brain is absorbing. There is a key to the listening exercises (pages 45–47) to help you with these, but try to do them by ear first. Once you start to really hear the music, you'll be glad you did.

In addition to the listening exercises, the CD includes all of the examples in the book and also play-along tracks for practicing your soloing. Go through the book at your own pace. It is better to learn a concept well, apply it to many keys, and really hear it, rather than spread yourself too thin.

As you learn to solo, remember to listen; it is the single most important skill for improvisation. How many of the concepts from this book can you hear on CDs, records, or in live performances? Listen for and learn new ideas that are not in this book. Finally, don't forget to try out your ideas with other musicians. Get together with your friends and jam, or find sessions where you can sit in. The more you play solos, the more comfortable you'll become, and the more fun you'll have. Happy improvising!

MUSIC REVIEW

Middle C

Let's start by finding *middle C* on the keyboard. There are eight C's on a full keyboard. You can locate them using the pattern of black notes. The black notes are grouped into twos and threes. First, look for a group of two black notes. C is the white note just to the left of the two black notes. Middle C is the C closest to the center of the keyboard, usually underneath the instrument's brand name.

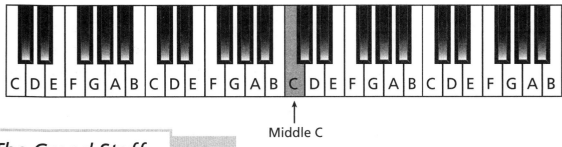

Middle C

The Grand Staff

Middle C gets its name, however, not from its location on the keyboard, but from where it falls on the *grand staff*.

The Grand Staff

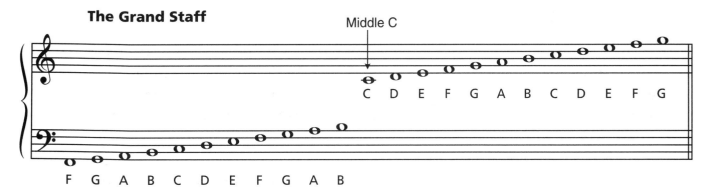

The grand staff is used to notate piano music. It is comprised of two groups of horizontal lines, with a space between them. Each group contains five lines and displays the notes to be played by one of your hands. The top group, called the *treble clef* 𝄞, displays right-hand notes; the bottom group, called the *bass clef* 𝄢, displays left-hand notes. Since this book is about soloing, and you do that mostly with your right hand, we'll generally be displaying the right hand, or treble clef parts, rather than the grand staff.

Middle C sits right in between the bass and treble clef and has its own *ledger line,* which connects the two halves of the grand staff.

All the notes on the grand staff are labeled using the letters A, B, C, D, E, F, and G. These seven letters make up the *musical alphabet*. Put your thumb on middle C. If you ascend the keyboard, playing only white notes, you'll play C, D, E, F, G, A, B, then you start over (C, D, E, etc.). So there are only seven white notes to learn—that's not so bad.

Sharps and Flats

What about the black notes in between? They represent the *sharps* and *flats*. A black note above, or to the right, of a white note is a *sharp* (♯).

A black note below, or to the left, of a white note is a *flat* (♭).

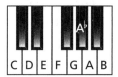

Did you notice that the same key might have two different note names, such as G♯ and A♭? How it's labeled depends on its function in a chord or a scale—more on that later.

Half Steps and Whole Steps

When we talk about *soloing* in the blues, we'll use some numbers to describe which notes we're playing. The numbers describe *intervals,* which refer to the distance between two notes, and/or to a note's position in a major scale. Let's clarify this by looking at some intervals and building a major scale.

The smallest interval is a *half step*. This is the distance between two notes on the piano, which are as close to each other as possible. For example:

B and C

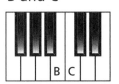

F and F♯

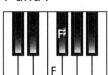

C♯ and D

In each case, there is no other note between the two notes named. Notice the two places on the keyboard where there are half steps between two white notes: B–C and E–F.

A *whole step* is the distance between two notes with one note between them. It is also equal to two half steps. For example:

G and A

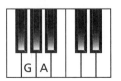

G♭ and A♭

B and C♯

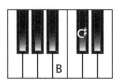

A whole step can be between two white notes, two black notes, or a white note and a black note.

Note: Interval names, such as "half step" or "minor 3rd," can refer to distances above *or* below a note.

The Major Scale

The *major scale* is based on a specific pattern of whole steps and half steps. It is the foundation for most Western music. You may know it as Do–Re–Mi–Fa–So–La–Ti–Do. The pattern of steps is: Whole–Whole–Half–Whole–Whole–Whole–Half. Starting on C, this pattern produces the C Major scale, which is all white notes:

C Major Scale

D Major Scale

Starting the pattern on any other note yields a mixture of black and white notes. Here's a D Major Scale, which starts on the note D.

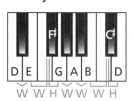

When we talk about improvising, we use numbers to indicate *degrees* of the major scale: 1-2-3-4-5-6-7. So, is we are talking about the D Major scale, we say D is the *1st degree* of the scale, E is the *2nd degree*, and so forth. The first degree is also called the *tonic*—so D is the tonic of the D Major scale.

Chords

Chords are collections of notes formed by taking every *other* note from a scale. *Triads* are chords containing three notes. *Major triads* are formed by taking the 1st, 3rd, and 5th degrees of the major scale. For example, a D Major scale is: D(1)–E(2)–F♯(3)–G(4)–A(5)–B(6)–C(7). So, a D Major triad is: D(1)–F♯(3)–A(5).

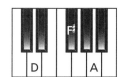

To make a *minor triad*, lower the 3rd degree by a half step: D–F–A is a D Minor triad.

Another way to build triads is by knowing the interval between each note in the chord. The interval between the first two notes in a major triad is a *major 3rd*. It's made up of four half steps or two whole steps.

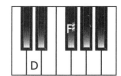

The interval between the next two notes of the triad is a *minor 3rd*. Its size is three half steps or one whole step plus one half step.

In a minor triad, the interval between the first two notes is a minor 3rd. The interval between the top two notes is a major 3rd.

Listening Exercise 1

Listen to Track 1 on the CD. You'll hear two notes played, then repeated. Identify the interval between the two notes. Is it a half step, whole step, minor 3rd, or major 3rd?

INGREDIENTS FOR A 12-BAR BLUES

Blues music can come in many forms. A blues can be major or minor, slow or up-tempo, swinging or funky, and harmonically simple or complicated. But most of the time, when musicians say "let's play a blues," they're referring to songs based on a common 12-bar structure, which, in its simplest version, uses only three chords.

Here is a simple blues in C. Your left hand plays the *root* of each chord (the root is the note on which the chord is built), while your right hand plays major triads. Play through the example below.

2 SIMPLE BLUES IN C

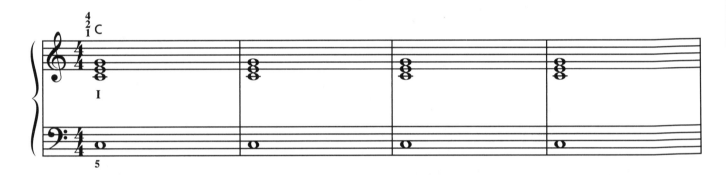

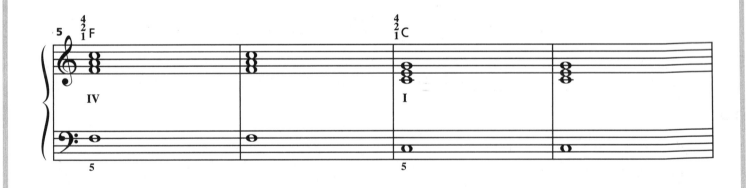

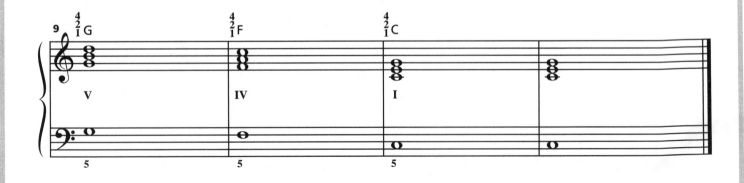

On page 7, we saw that the notes in a scale are given numbers to describe their position in the scale. We can use those numbers to understand the blues form in any key.

For example, in the key of C, the "one" chord is C Major. (It's built by starting on C and taking every other note of the scale: C–E–G.) Roman numerals are used to label the function of a chord, so C is the *I chord* ("one" chord). Upper-case Roman numerals are used to designate major chords, and lower-case Roman numerals are used to designate minor chords. For example, the second chord from the C Major scale is built starting from D and taking every other note of the scale: D–F–A. It is called a D Minor triad and is referred to as the *ii chord* ("two" chord). The diagram to the right illustrates the function of each triad built from the C Major scale.

F is the 4th degree of the C Major scale, so F Major is the *IV chord* in the key of C.

G is the 5th degree of the C Major scale, so G Major is the *V chord* in the key of C.

We can play a 12-bar blues in any key using the I, IV, and V chords from that key.

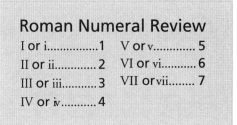

Roman Numeral Review

I or i	1	V or v	5
II or ii	2	VI or vi	6
III or iii	3	VII or vii	7
IV or iv	4		

The following chord chart shows a 12-bar blues using Roman numerals for the I ("one"), IV ("four"), and V ("five") chords.

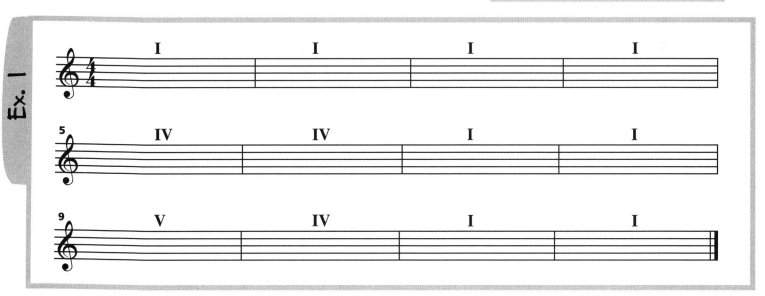

Let's find the I, IV and V chords in the key of F and play an F blues. To the right is an F Major scale:

The I chord is F Major, the IV chord is B♭ Major, and the V chord is C Major. Inserting each chord into the form where it belongs gives us the chord progression in F.

In this example, your right hand is playing triads again, while your left hand plays a *shuffle pattern*. The rhythmic foundation of a shuffle is *eighth-note triplets*. This means there are three eighth notes played in each beat (instead of two). The shuffle pattern sounds like eighth-note triplets with the first two tied together but is written as regular eighth notes, with the marking *Swing 8ths* at the start of the piece.

Listen to Track 3 on the CD to hear an example of the drums playing a shuffle beat, followed by drums, bass, and piano. Make sure you can hear the larger beat "1, 2, 3, 4" as well as the triplet within each beat, which is usually counted "1 and a, 2 and a, 3 and a, 4 and a."

Easy Soloing for Blues Keyboard will focus primarily on learning to improvise with your right hand. If you don't already have favorite ways of accompanying yourself, try the left hand part in this example. It's easy to learn in any key and is a good place to start.

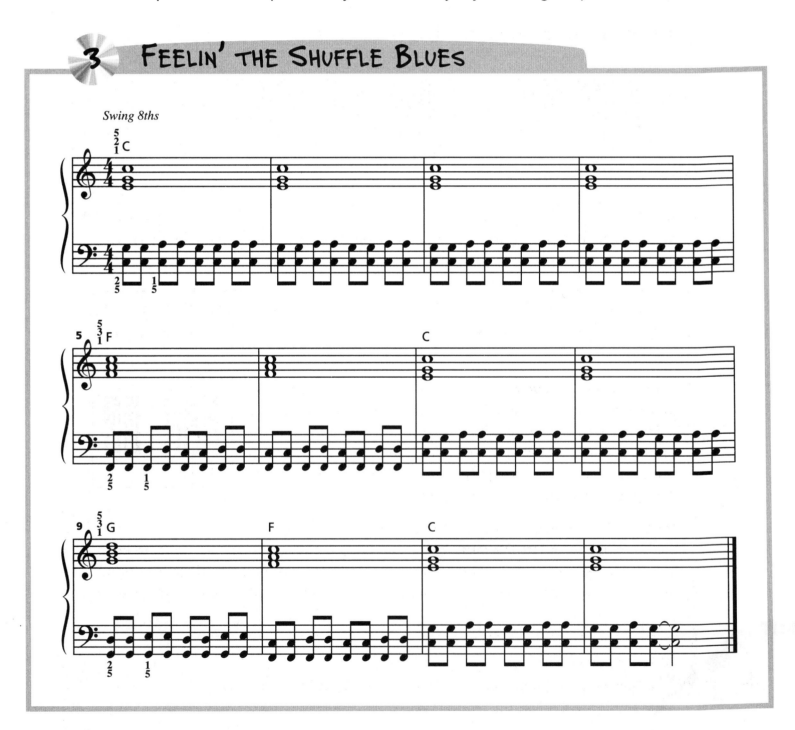

3 FEELIN' THE SHUFFLE BLUES

Dominant Chords

So far, we've been playing the blues with triads, but 12-bar blues are generally played with chords like C7, F7, and G7. These chords have four notes and are called *dominant chords.* To build a dominant chord, start with a major triad and stack a minor 3rd on top of it:

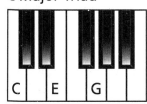

C Major Triad

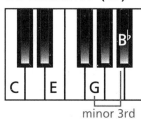

C Dominant 7 (C7)

Using this same logic, we can construct the F7 and G7 chords:

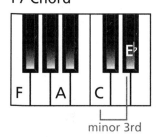

F7 Chord

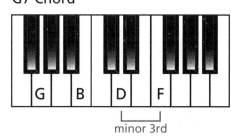

G7 Chord

Another way to build a dominant chord is by taking the R, 3rd, 5th, and 7th of a major scale and lowering the 7th by a half-step (indicated with $^\flat$7):

C Major Scale	C	D	E	F	G	A	B
	R	2	3	4	5	6	7

C7 Chord	C	E	G	B$^\flat$
	R	3	5	$^\flat$7

F7 Chord

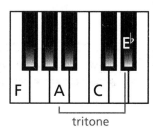

Dominant chords have a very particular sound. They are neither totally major nor totally minor. The interval formed by the 3rd and $^\flat$7 of the chord is a *tritone.* It is equal to three whole steps. The tritone is a very unstable interval that wants to *resolve.* In other words, the music wants to go forward to find a resting place. To the right is an F7 chord with the tritone indicated.

The blues form is unique because all of the chords are dominant— the harmony never lets the music come to a complete rest, but instead wants to keep going around, *chorus* after chorus. (A chorus is one complete time through the form.) Dominant chords are an important part of the blues' emotionally charged character.

Listening Exercise 2

Listen to Track 4 and identify each chord you hear as being a major triad, minor triad, or dominant chord.

Since the tritone formed by the 3rd and 7th is the interval that really gives the dominant chord its character, all that's really needed for a great left-hand blues piano accompaniment is the 3rd and 7th of each dominant chord.

In a C blues, the first chord is C7: C–E–G–B♭. The 3rd is E and the 7th is B♭. Play E and B♭ in your left hand, and with your right hand, reach down and play a low C. This is your voicing for a C7 chord.

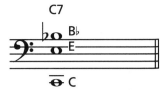

Your right hand is taking the place of the bass player at the moment. When you improvise, your right hand will play melodies, your left hand will play the 3rd and 7th of the chord, and a bass player will play the roots for you.

Now let's look at F7: F–A–C–E♭. The 3rd is A and the 7th is E♭:

Here's a trick: When we voice chords on the piano, the notes can be in any order. Let's flip the order of the 3rd and 7th, placing the A above the E♭.

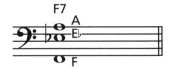

Look how close together the voicings for C7 and F7 have become. To go from C7 to F7 (the I chord to the IV chord), just move each note down by a half step.

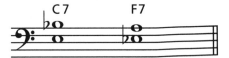

The third chord in our C blues is G. The 3rd is B and the 7th is F. We'll flip the order of this one too, placing the B over the F.

To move from the I chord to the V chord, just move each note up a half step. To move from the V chord to the IV chord, move each note down a whole step.

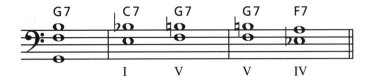

Exercise

Following the 12-bar blues form introduced on page 8, and using the concepts above, play 3rds and 7ths in your left hand for a blues in C. If you need help figuring out the chord voicings, look ahead to the left-hand part in "Two Is Enough" (page 14).

IMPROVISING: TELLING YOUR OWN STORY

It's time to start soloing over the blues. As you go through the rest of this book, you will learn about different scales, chords, and rhythms. More importantly, you will learn to "talk" through the piano. You will be finding a way to tell your own story through your instrument.

The blues are all about people telling stories. Before guitars, pianos, and saxophones, people used their voices and simple drums to "talk" musically about their experiences. We have to remember this when we improvise, because more important than the notes we play, is how well we communicate our story.

Here's an example of a blues lyric:

I got runnin', I got runnin' on my brain
I got runnin', I got runnin' on my brain
Hate to leave you baby, but you makes me so insane

We already know that a typical blues chorus is 12 bars long. Now we can also see that within those 12 bars is a pattern. The first line of lyrics (4 bars) starts the story, the second line (4 bars) repeats it, and the third line (4 bars) finishes it. If we remember this storytelling quality when we improvise, we can make even the simplest solo sound great.

Soloing with Just Two Notes

Here's an example of a blues chorus, played with just two notes, the root and the ♭3 of the key.

5 LIVE AT THE TWO-NOTE

The solo sounded convincing, even though it is simple enough for anyone to play. Let's see why:

1. There is a clear idea that is stated and repeated.
2. There is space between ideas.
3. The solo follows the AAB pattern of typical blues lyrics (first four measures are repeated, then answered with a different third line).

Following is another example of a two-note blues. This tune is also in the key of C and uses only the root and the 5th: C and G. It's inspired by a famous Duke Ellington song called "C Jam Blues." The left-hand part is shown here as well, playing 3rds and 7ths. You can practice playing along to Track 6, with or without playing the left-hand part. On the CD, the form is played three times. The first time through, the solo is played as written. The band plays for two more choruses so you can practice improvising your own two-note solo.

6 TWO IS ENOUGH

Listening Exercise 3

Listen to Track 7. Play along with the 12-bar blues in C, listening to the two-note ideas and playing them back in the spaces. (Hint: Every idea uses either the root and ♭3rd, or the root and 5th of the key.)

Soloing with Three Notes

Now, let's use a three-note idea to tell a story. This time we'll play in the key of F. This example uses the root, ♭3rd, and 4th: F–A♭–B♭. Try playing just your right hand alone, or try adding 3rds and 7ths in your left hand. Practice the solo as written, then try improvising your own solo as the band repeats the form two more times.

8 THREE'S COMPANY

Another three notes you can combine for great blues ideas are the 5, the ♭7, and the root. For the key of F, the three notes would be C–E♭–F.

Check out these different "motifs" using C–E♭–F:

9

Ex. 2

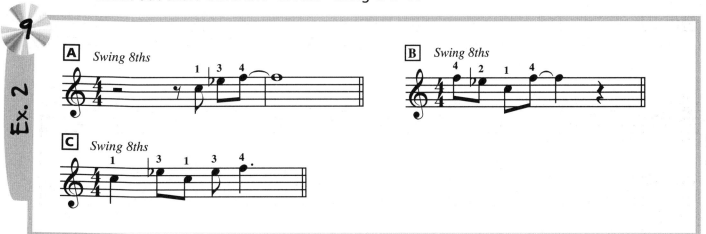

10 **L**istening Exercise 4

Listen to Track 10. Repeat these three-note ideas built from the root, ♭3, and 4; or the 5, ♭7, and root. The key of each idea will be identified before the idea is played.

The following blues tune is in the key of G and uses both of our three-note ideas: R–♭3–4 and 5–♭7–R. Play the solo as written, then try improvising your own.

11 2 X 3

12 **L**istening Exercise 5
Track 12 features two more choruses of blues in F. Listen to the three-note ideas and play them back in the spaces.

You now have a lot of "words" in your blues vocabulary, so it's time to start talking. Your words are the two- and three-note ideas we've been working with. You'll make sentences by putting the ideas together into longer musical phrases, and you'll tell stories by putting those phrases together into blues choruses. Here are a few things to think about when you tell your story:

1. **Leave space.** When we speak, we pause between phrases and sentences. If we didn't, no one would listen to us for very long.

2. **Use repetition.** Saying something more than once helps the listener to really hear it, and helps you make your point.

3. **The root is home base.** Ending an idea with the root is like coming home. (In musical language, we call this *resolving*.) Starting on the root and ending somewhere else is like going away from home (unresolved). When you play ideas, try to notice whether they sound resolved or not so you can express yourself exactly as you want.

Combining Two-Note and Three-Note Ideas

We can make longer words or phrases just by combining two- and three-note ideas. Example 3A combines a two-note idea with a three-note idea. Example 3B combines two three-note ideas in a row.

The following blues chorus in C uses both of the ideas shown above. Play the solo as written, then try using these ideas to come up with your own solo.

Here are some more combinations of two- and three-note ideas for a blues in C. For each one, do the following:

1. Memorize the idea.

2. Identify which scale degree the idea starts on (R, ♭3, 4, 5, or ♭7).

3. Transpose the idea into two other keys.

THE MINOR PENTATONIC AND BLUES SCALES

The Minor Pentatonic Scale

So far, you've been playing ideas using a few specific notes related to the key in which you're playing. You've used the root, $\flat$3rd, and 4th, as well as the 5th and $\flat$7th. If you put all of these notes together, they collectively form a scale called the *minor pentatonic scale*. The formula for the minor pentatonic scale is: R–$\flat$3–4–5–$\flat$7. The C Minor Pentatonic scale, for example, is: C–E$\flat$–F–G–B$\flat$ (see right).

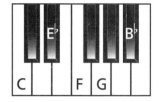

You can use the notes of the minor pentatonic scale to solo over the blues. What's important, though, is that you *hear* the ideas you are playing. That's why it's a good idea to spend time playing two- and three-note ideas. As your ears begin to understand how the different notes of the minor pentatonic scale go together to form ideas, you can use the notes to play solos that say what you want to say.

The Blues Scale

If we add a $\flat$5 to the minor pentatonic scale, we get the *blues scale*. In some styles of blues, even master players use only the notes from the blues scale for their improvisations. The formula for the blues scale is: R–$\flat$3–4–$\flat$5–5–$\flat$7. The C Blues scale, for example is: C–E$\flat$–F–G$\flat$–G–B$\flat$ (see right).

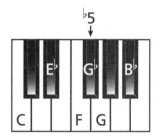

Try playing this popular blues lick, which descends part of the blues scale.

Here is a chorus of blues in G featuring the descending blues lick at the bottom of page 19.

17 FLAT CITY BLUES

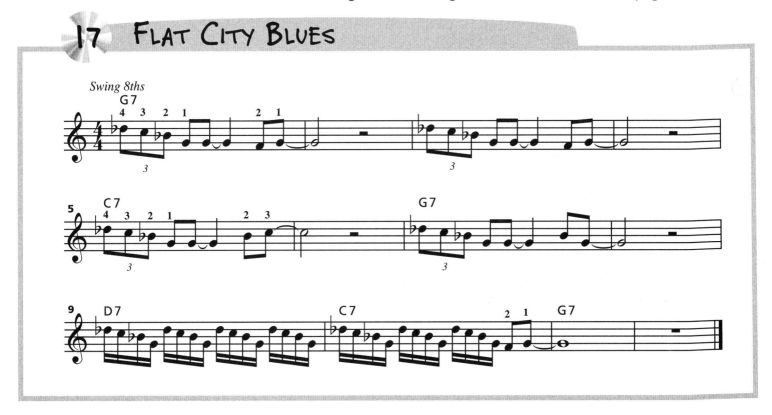

Let's look at a few more classic blues ideas that use the ♭5. (Note: Writing the D♭ as a C♯ makes the line easier to read, since the D♭ or C♯ is followed by a D♮.)

18
Ex. 6

19

Listening Exercise 6
Listen to Track 19. Repeat each ♭5 idea that you hear. The key of each idea will be identified before it's played.

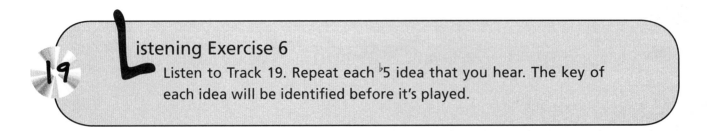

Another popular way of using the blues scale to make a melody is simply to play it from top to bottom.

Practice descending the C Blues scale, using the fingering suggested below.

20

Ex. 7

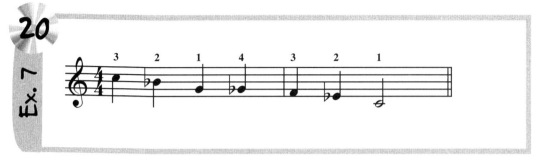

You can use the above fingering to descend the blues scale in any key.

For a great example of the descending blues scale played as a melody, find a recording of Sonny Rollins's jazz blues "Sonny Moon for Two." Below is a similar blues in the key of B♭. Notice that there is an E♭7 in the second measure. This is called a *quick four*, meaning that there is a change to the IV chord in the second measure of the form. The I chord returns in the third measure and the rest of the 12-bar form remains the same.

21 ## GOING DOWNSTAIRS

Exercise

22

Try playing the descending B♭ Blues scale over Track 22, starting on different beats, using different rhythms, and repeating notes. Let your ears be your guide. What do you think sounds cool?

Up to now, we've been playing over blues tunes built with dominant chords, but the blues can also be built entirely from minor chords. Lower case Roman numerals indicate minor chords, so the chords of a minor blues are i, iv, and v instead of I, IV, and V. The blues scale works perfectly for improvising over them. Here is an example of a solo on a D Minor blues, using the D Blues scale. Memorize some of the ideas in the solo and try playing them in other keys.

23 It's All Downhill

GETTING MORE MILEAGE OUT OF YOUR IDEAS

We've learned the blues scale and can use it to play great melodies over a regular 12-bar or a minor blues. Now, it's time to do more than just play melodies using the scale. Some of the greatest blues players, particularly of Chicago-style blues, can take extended, dramatic, virtuosic solos using only the blues scale. Let's take a look at a few ways in which they take the ingredients of the blues scale and put them together to sound great.

Play Clusters from the Scale in Repeating Patterns

Back when great piano players like Otis Spann and Pinetop Perkins were playing in clubs with bandleaders like Muddy Waters, they had upright pianos which were often not very well amplified, and they were playing with loud electric guitars, basses, and drums. Some of the cool stylistic things they did resulted from their desire to be heard. One such device was playing repeated blues-scale clusters. On a blues in A, for example, Otis Spann might have played a figure like this:

Let's see what notes are in the cluster. G is the ♭7th of the key. E is the 5th of the key. D♯ is the same as E♭, the ♭5th of the key. Playing all three notes at the same time creates an edgy sound that "cuts" through what the other instruments are doing. The strong rhythm of the *quarter-note triplets* also helps the part to stand out.

Quarter-Note Triplets

Quarter-note triplets sound great over a shuffle because they work *with* and *against* the rhythm that the other instruments are playing. On page 10, we looked at a shuffle pattern and got familiar with the feeling of eighth-note triplets. To play quarter-note triplets, you simply play every other note in the eighth-note triplets (see below).

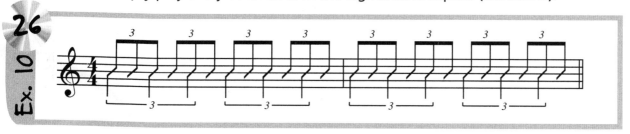

Rhythm, Rhythm, Rhythm

The triplet feeling can be a great source for rhythmic ideas in your soloing. Following are some exercises to help you to be rhythmically solid and creative when you play.

1. Practice alternating measures of quarter notes and eighth-note triplets.

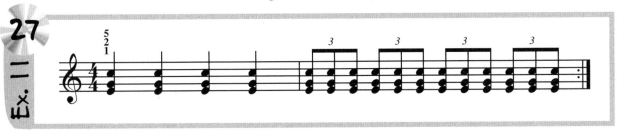

2. Now, practice playing two beats of each.

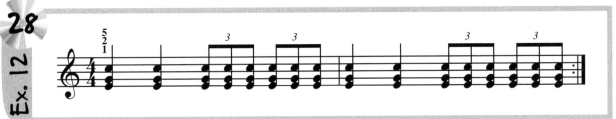

3. Play four measures of eighth-note triplets, accenting every other one.

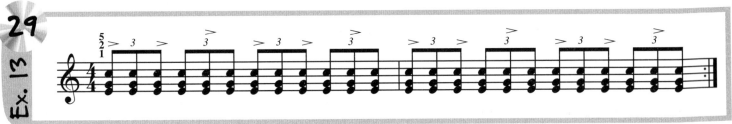

4. Alternate measures of eighth-note triplets and quarter-note triplets.

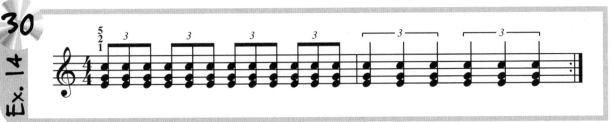

Exercise

Play your own rhythmic patterns using a mixture of quarter notes, quarter-note triplets, and eighth-note triplets. Choose a cluster of notes from the blues scale and take it through each of your new rhythms.

Add the Root or the 5th Above Your Ideas

Another way to make simple blues-scale ideas sound great is to add the root or the 5th of the scale as a constant note over the idea.

Let's look at an example.

31

Ex. 15

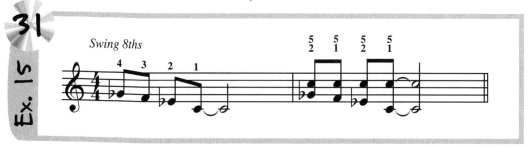

Here is another example of a blues idea in the key of F, with the root repeated on top.

32

Ex. 16

In the examples below, the 5th is repeated over the top.

33

Ex. 17

34

Listening Exercise 7
Listen to Track 34. Each blues scale idea will be played and then repeated with either the root or the 5th above it. Listen to the ideas and play them back, both with and without the added note.

Here's a blues in F that's full of blues-scale ideas with the root or the 5th added on the top.

35 OVER THE TOP BLUES

Use Octaves to Emphasize Ideas

A simple melodic idea has more "oomph" when played in *octaves.* An octave is the interval between two notes of the same name, nearest to each other on the piano. For example, the distance between middle C and the next higher C on the piano is an octave. If you play both C's at one time and then continue up the C Major scale, playing D plus the next D above it, E plus the next E above it, and so forth, you are playing the C scale *in octaves.* Check out this blues scale phrase in the key of F using octaves.

36

Ex. 18

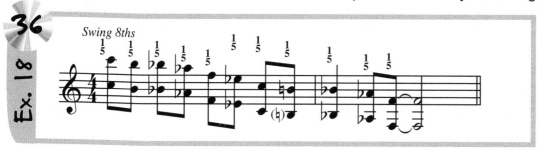

Use Trills to Create a Dramatic Effect

A *trill* consists of a rapid alternation between two notes. In classical music, most trills are between two adjacent notes. In the blues, you might trill between two notes from the blues scale. This just means to play one of the notes with your thumb and the other with your 2nd or 3rd finger and alternate between them as quickly as is comfortable for you. In written music, a trill is indicated by a "squiggly" line above the notes that are to be trilled. For instance, if you are in the key of F, you can trill on the root and the ♭3 (Ex. 19A) or the 5 and the ♭7 (Ex. 19B).

37

Ex. 19

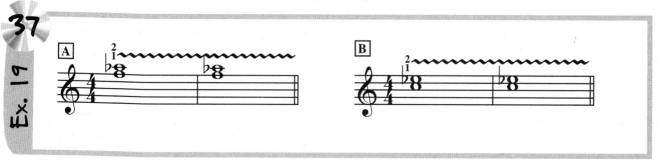

Take a Simple Idea and Repeat It Over Different Octaves

38

Ex. 20

It's great to be dramatic when you play the blues. Experiment with these ideas and techniques to see if you can come up with some of your own sensational signature blues expressions!

Here's a Chicago-style shuffle in the key of F. All of the material in the solo comes from the blues scale.

39 CHICAGO STYLE

PLAYING OFF THE CHORDS

Up to now, we've been working on playing melody-based ideas in our improvisations—ideas that can be played over an entire blues form without being altered to fit any specific chord. This is a great approach, but we can also base our soloing on particular chords in the blues form.

Here's a blues in A that uses only the notes from each of the three triads in the 12-bar form: A Major (A–C♯–E), D Major (D–F♯–A), and E Major (E–G♯–B). By using inversions of the chords, it's possible to make some great melodies with just these pitches.

40 TRIAD BLUES

Exercise
Pick a triad and play it in different inversions up and down the keyboard.
Try doing this in all 12 keys. Below is an example using an A Major triad.

41
Ex. 21

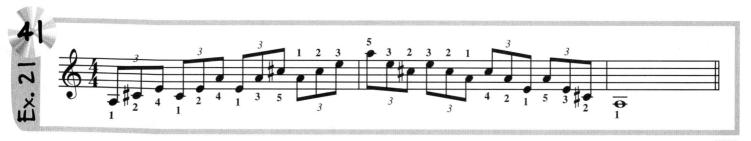

Now, let's make a melody that's built from a larger number of pitches than just triads. We will begin with the notes of a dominant chord. The notes in a C7 chord are C–E–G–B♭. We can arpeggiate the chord like this:

Now, let's add a note between the G and the B♭. This note, A, is called a *passing tone*.

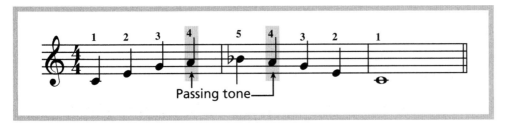

Passing tone

We can take this idea through each of the three chords in a blues, to end up with a melody like the following blues melody in the key of C.

42   PASSING TONE BLUES

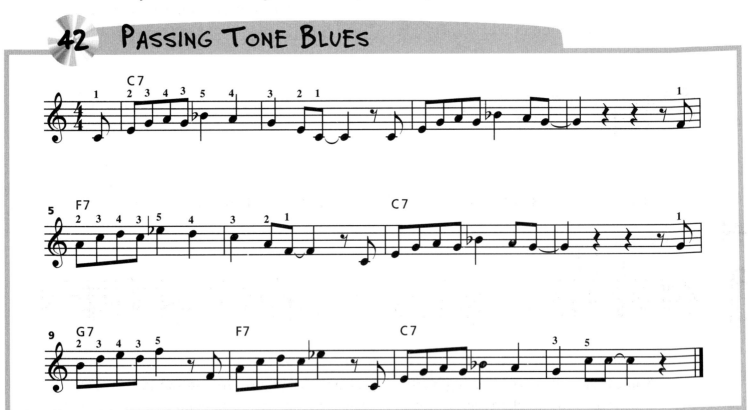

Listening Exercise 8

43   Listen to Track 43 and repeat the ideas made from chord tones. The chord from which the idea is built will be identified before the idea is played.

Another way you can use chords for soloing is to play figures off of the chords, like this basic idea which is sometimes called a *pull-off:*

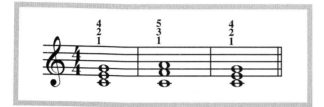

Here's how to play a pull-off:

1. Play the triad.

2. Keeping your thumb on the root, move the 3rd of the chord up to the 4th scale degree, and the 5th of the chord up to the 6th degree.

3. Return to the position of the regular triad. Sometimes, piano players like to mimic the sound of a guitar player *bending* the 3rd. On a keyboard you can do this by playing the ♭3 as a *grace note* and sliding off of it onto the major 3rd of the chord. A grace note embellishes the note that follows. It is played quickly, with no rhythmic value of its own. Grace notes are written as small notes with a slash through the note's flag (♪).

Here are four bars of the pull-off on a C triad played with a bent 3rd.

You can take this idea one step further by extending the upward motion to the root, 5th, and 7th of the dominant chord, as shown in the following example.

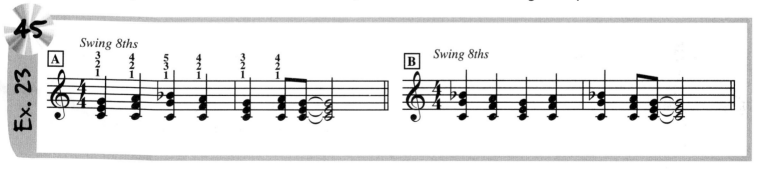

"The On-Again, Off-Again Blues" is a blues in G that puts the pull-off to good use. A G blues uses three chords: G7, C7, and D7. We already know what the pull-off looks like on a C chord. Let's figure it out for G7 and D7:

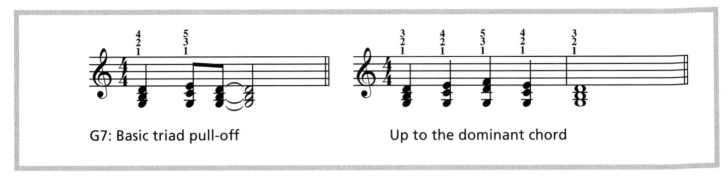

G7: Basic triad pull-off   Up to the dominant chord

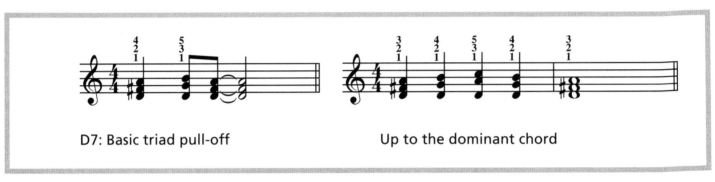

D7: Basic triad pull-off   Up to the dominant chord

46 THE ON-AGAIN, OFF-AGAIN BLUES

Approach Tones

Another way to enhance chord-tone melodies is by using *chromatic approach* tones. Approach tones are notes played before a chord tone as a melodic way of approaching them. *Chromatic* means to move by half-steps, so a chromatic approach tone is a note one half step above or below a chord tone. You can use chromatic approach tones to add tension or complexity to a chord-based melody.

Below is a simple example of a chromatic approach tone, which closely mimics a bent 3rd on a guitar. We're not giving the approach tone a very long rhythmic value, so it is notated as a grace note.

Here is a similar idea, again using the ♭3 as an approach to the 3rd, but this time giving it more rhythmic importance.

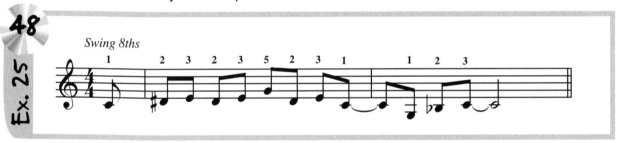

Following is an idea that uses approach tones to the 5th of the chord. Notice it uses two approach tones—the 6th followed by the ♭6th leading to the 5th. (This is sometimes called a *double-chromatic approach*.)

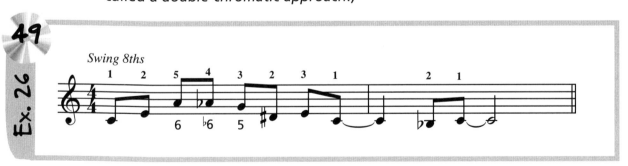

Here's a blues in F with a melody built from chord tones and chromatic approaches. The approach tones are highlighted. Note that the scale degree is labeled based on the chord that's being played at the time. For example, the C♯ (D♭ enharmonically) in measure 5 is ♭6 in the key of F, but is the ♭3 of the B♭ or IV chord.

50 APPROACHIN', ENROACHIN' BLUES

Did you notice that, in measures 8, 9, and 10, the approach tone occurs on the "and" of four in the measure before the chord changes? This is a device called *anticipation*, which is commonly used in music with a swing or shuffle feel. Including anticipation in your improvisation will add to the overall energy of the music.

Chord-Tone Exercise

This is a great exercise for getting roots, 3rds, 5ths, and 7ths under your fingers. It's written in the key of C, but try playing it in other keys too.

So far, we've approached improvising in two ways:

1. By playing ideas from the blues scale over the whole blues form
2. By playing melodies based on chord tones

There is a third approach to improvising on the blues, which combines elements from the first two. It involves playing an idea over the first chord and then changing it just a little to fit the next chord in the form.

Let's look at an example of this on a blues in C. The chord changes to this blues include an F7 in the second measure, known as a quick four (see page 21). The I chord returns in the 3rd measure, and the rest of the 12-bar form remains the same. Some blues tunes have quick fours, and some don't. You can train your ears to hear the difference.

52 MAKIN' CHANGES BLUES

We started with an idea based on the C7 chord. When we arrive at the IV chord, F7, we could have transposed the melodic shape, starting on the 3rd of F7, but instead, we kept our idea almost the same, just changing it a little to fit F7 rather than C7.

The E in the C7 idea doesn't fit with an F7 (F–A–C–E♭), so it becomes E♭. Now the idea works over F7:

When we get to the G7 chord, a new idea is introduced. That idea is then transposed downward to fit over the F7 that follows.

Ex. 29

Exercise

Each of the followings ideas fits over the *I* chord of the given key. Change each idea just enough to make it fit over the *IV* chord of the corresponding key.

Here's an example in the key of G:

53

Ex. 30

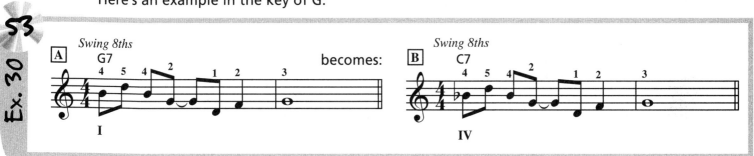

Now try the exercise based on the following examples. (IV-chord licks are upside-down.)

Ex. 31

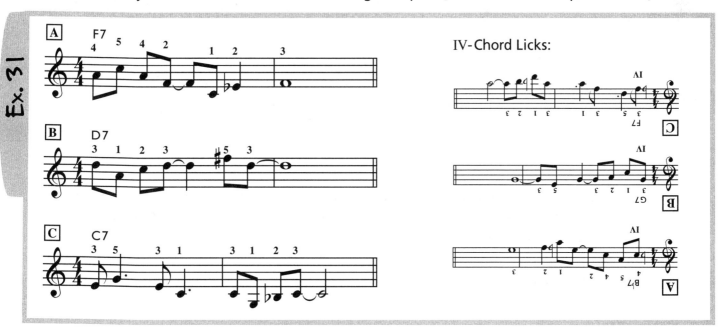

Listening Exercise 9

54

Listen to each idea in Track 54 and repeat it. Then, listen to how it is changed to fit the IV chord and repeat the new shape.

More About the V Chord

By now, you're probably getting quite good at changing I chord ideas to fit over the IV chord. That will take you through the first eight measures of a blues, but what happens after that? The most important thing to remember when coming to the end of a blues chorus is to use your ears. By the time you get to measure 9, you've been groovin' on a theme for eight measures. If you've been listening to what you're playing, you will probably "hear" a potential conclusion to your 12-bar statement. As you saw on "Makin' Changes Blues," introducing a new idea over the V chord can sound great.

On the other hand, you might want to continue with the same idea that you played over the I and IV chords. Here's an example:

55 HIGH FIVE BLUES

The melody played over the V chord is the same as over the I chord, but with a D (the 5th of G7) substituting for the note C, and a B (the 3rd of G7) substituting for the note B♭.

Playing Over Turnarounds and *ii–V7* Progressions

Some 12-bar blues forms have more complex chord structures. They might include a ii–V–I progression in the last four measures, for instance. In the jazz idiom, this is very common. Here's an example in the key of C:

56
Ex. 32

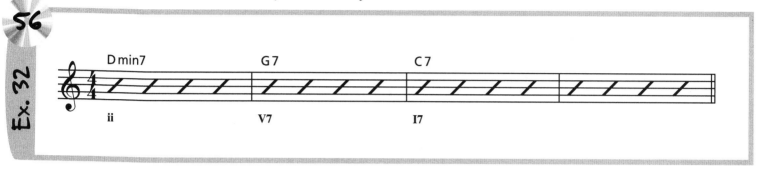

Or, the first four measures might contain a quick four followed by a ii-V progression leading to the IV chord. This device is also commonly found in jazz-style blues.

57
Ex. 33

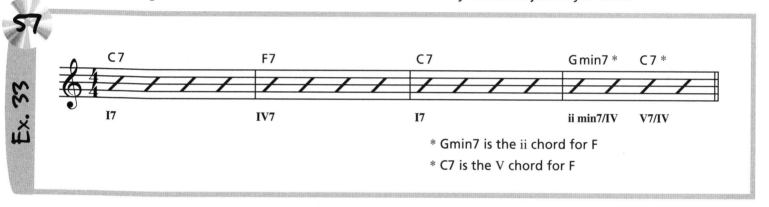

* Gmin7 is the ii chord for F
* C7 is the V chord for F

There could be any number of chord progressions in the last two measures of the form. These progressions are called *turnarounds*, because their function is to return you to the beginning of the form. The turnaround might be as simple as a V7 chord played on beats 3 and 4 of the final measure:

58
Ex. 34

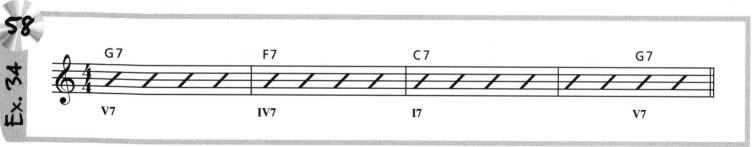

Or, it might be another ii–V progression, this time preceded by a VI7 chord as well.

59
Ex. 35

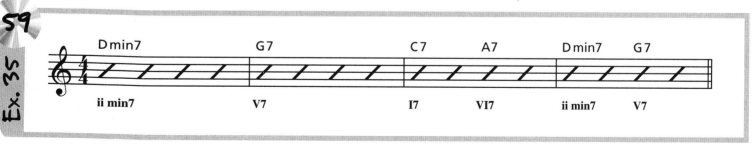

Most of the time, you can let the extra chord changes and complex turnarounds go by without really worrying about them. For instance, Example 59 (page 39) can be treated like a big long C7 chord. This is because the blues is all about melodic ideas, not necessarily following every single chord change. You can play all of your cool C7 ideas over the whole phrase and they will sound great:

Turnaround Exercises

Below are four different chord progressions for measures 9–12 of a G blues. Play along with the tracks, trying out your different soloing ideas to see which you like best over each progression.

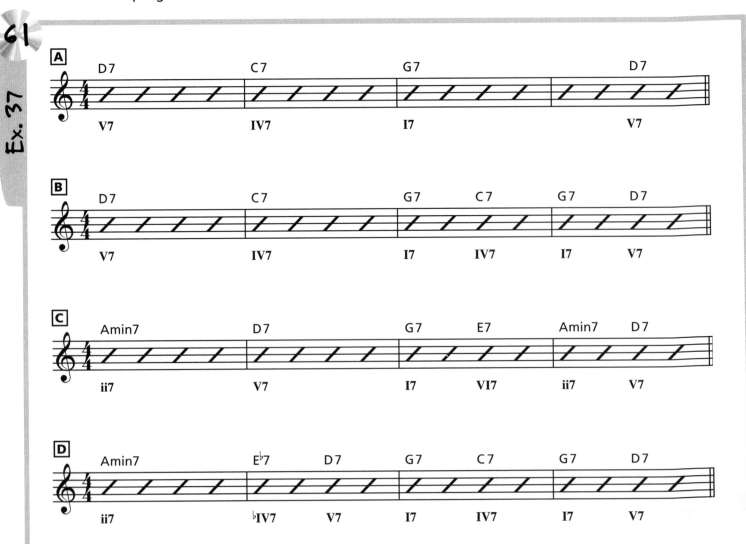

PUTTING IT ALL TOGETHER FOR THE HIPPEST SOUND

It's time to start playing some really great blues solos. You can take your improvising to the next level by simply combining some of the ideas you've already worked on. Check out this blues in G, and see if you recognize some of the ideas.

62 TOGETHER FOREVER BLUES

The phrases are made up of blues-scale ideas, combined with chord-based ideas. Combining the two different sounds into one line makes the phrase really interesting.

Ex. 38

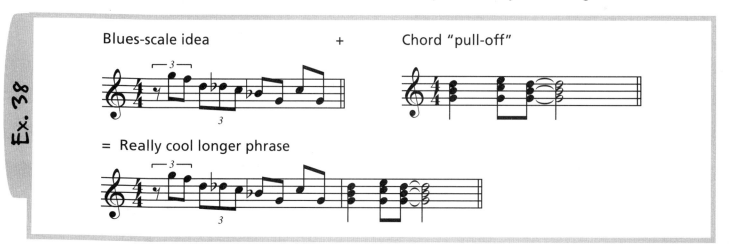

Blues-scale idea   +   Chord "pull-off"

= Really cool longer phrase

The Balloon Approach

Another way to expand and lengthen your ideas is to "blow them up like a balloon."

You can start, for example, by repeating a short blues-scale idea:

Then, repeat it again with a few extra notes added on:

Repeat it again, with a longer blues-scale idea attached:

And yet again, with a different ending:

Until the balloon is full:

Here's how it turns out.

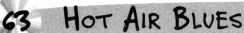

63 HOT AIR BLUES

Exercise

For each idea below, play the idea, then repeat it with three different endings.

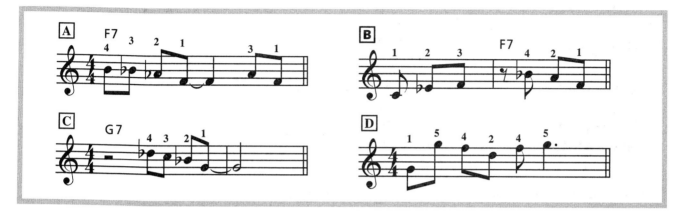

Now take one of the ideas from above and try developing it through a blues chorus. Write it down below.

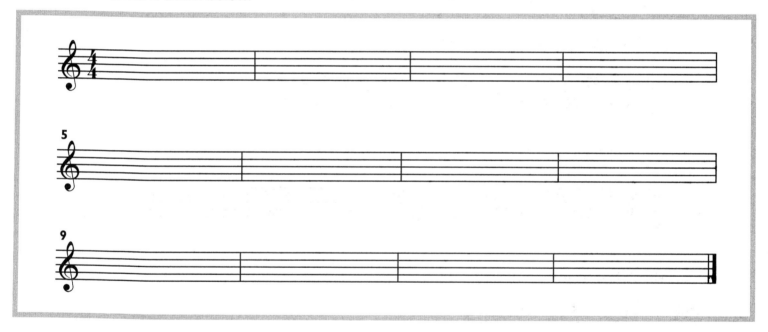

Listening Exercise 10

Listen to Track 64 and repeat each idea as new information is added.

Repeat, Combine, Extend

Let's focus on taking a more extended solo. Use repetition, idea combination, and the balloon approach to expand your ideas into an extended solo. On the next page is a blues solo that starts with a simple idea that is expanded in different ways, becoming more complex as the choruses go by. As you play the solo, see how much of the material you recognize. Which concepts and ideas from this book do you find in each chorus?

CONCLUSION:
ENOUGH ALREADY, TIME TO JAM!

Easy Soloing for Blues Keyboard has hopefully provided you with some great ideas for soloing and some exercises for getting your improvisational tools together. Now, it's time for you to take the next steps—play and listen, and listen and play. It's great to know the notes of a chord or the blues scale, but unless you listen to the blues, you won't really sound like a blues player. And unless you play your ideas a lot, you won't be able to make them come out right. So, now it's time to get your feet wet. Jam with your friends, listen to CDs, go out and sit in at clubs, and practice your ideas over and over.

As a little inspirational gift to get you going, you are being provided with your own private blues session, which you can do in your room, with nobody listening. Tracks 66–68 feature the rhythm section laying down the blues in three popular keys for you to play over. Happy jamming!

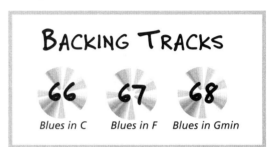

BACKING TRACKS

66   67   68

Blues in C   *Blues in F*   *Blues in Gmin*

Key to Listening Exercises

Listening Exercise 1: Major 3rd; minor 3rd; half step; major 3rd; whole step; minor 3rd; half step; whole step.

Listening Exercise 2: Dominant; minor; major; minor; dominant; major; dominant; minor.

Listening Exercise 3: Two blues choruses (six ideas per chorus).

Listening Exercise 4: Six short ideas using R, ♭3, 4 or 5, ♭7, R (identify key first).

12 Listening Exercise 5: Two blues choruses using three-note ideas.

19 Listening Exercise 6: Six short ♭5 ideas.

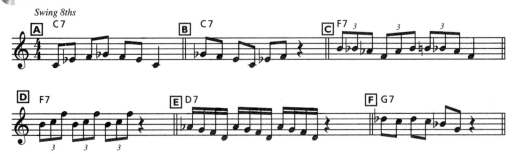

34 Listening Exercise 7: Four blues-scale ideas played then repeated with root or 5th above.

Listening Exercise 8: Four chord-tone ideas.

54 **Listening Exercise 9:** Four ideas played over the I chord, then changed to fit the IV chord.

64 **Listening Exercise 10:** Two ideas that are developed via balloon method.